EASY GUITAR WITH NOTES & TAB

# 4 CHORD ROCK

ISBN 978-1-4234-9237-5

HAL•LEONARD® CORPORATION

7777 W. BLUEMOUND RD. P.O. BOX 13819 MILWAUKEE, WI 53213

Visit Hal Leonard Online at
**www.halleonard.com**

# STRUM AND PICK PATTERNS

This chart contains the suggested strum and pick patterns that are referred to by number at the beginning of each song in this book. The symbols ⊓ and ∨ in the strum patterns refer to down and up strokes, respectively. The letters in the pick patterns indicate which right-hand fingers play which strings.

p = thumb
i = index finger
m = middle finger
a = ring finger

For example; Pick Pattern 2
is played: thumb - index - middle - ring

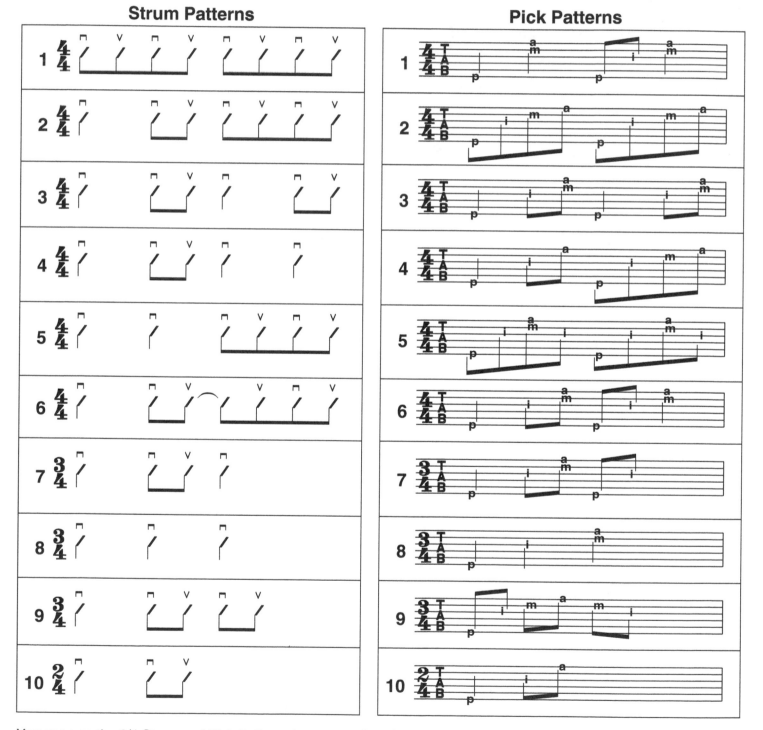

You can use the 3/4 Strum and Pick Patterns in songs written in compound meter (6/8, 9/8, 12/8, etc.).
For example, you can accompany a song in 6/8 by playing the 3/4 pattern twice in each measure.
The 4/4 Strum and Pick Patterns can be used for songs written in cut time (¢) by doubling the note time values in the patterns. Each pattern would therefore last two measures in cut time.

# Brown Eyed Girl

**Words and Music by Van Morrison**

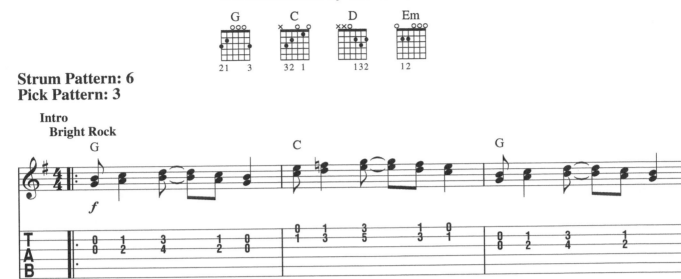

**Strum Pattern: 6**
**Pick Pattern: 3**

Intro
Bright Rock

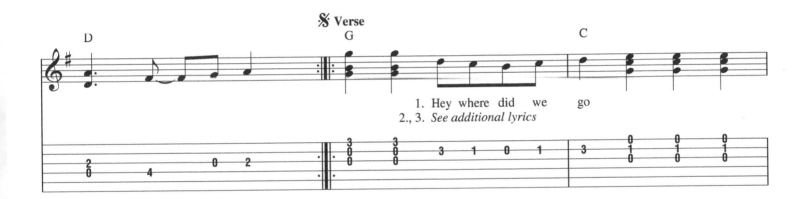

1. Hey where did we go
2., 3. *See additional lyrics*

days when the rains ___ came,      down in the hol -

low,      play-in' a new ___ game.      Laugh-in' and a

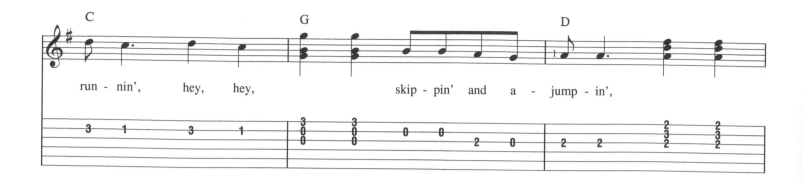

run-nin', hey, hey, skip-pin' and a-jump-in',

in the mist-y morn-ing fog with our hearts a thump-in' and

**Pre-Chorus**

you my brown eyed girl.

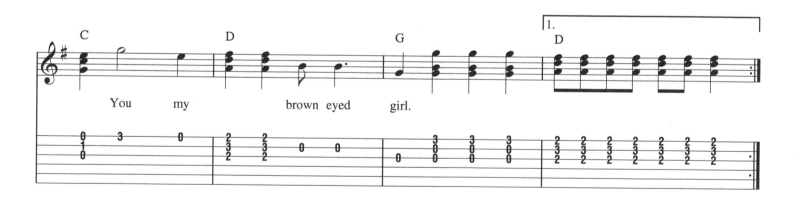

You my brown eyed girl.

Do you re-mem-ber when we used to sing?

**Chorus**

Sha, la, la, la, la, la, la, la, la, la, la, te da.

Sha, la, la, la, la, la, la, la,

la, la, la, te da. La, te da.

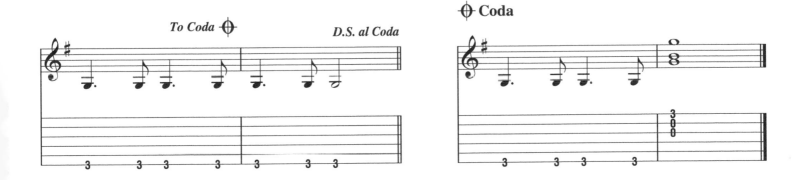

*Additional Lyrics*

2. Whatever happened
   To Tuesday and so slow,
   Going down the old mine
   With a transistor radio?
   Standin' in the sunlight laughin',
   Hiding behind a rainbow's wall,
   Slippin' and a slidin'
   All along the waterfall with you,
   My brown eyed girl,
   You, my brown eyed girl.

3. So hard to find my way
   Now that I'm all on my own.
   I saw you just the other day
   My, how you have grown.
   Cast my memory back there Lord,
   Sometimes I'm overcome thinkin' 'bout it.
   Laughin' and a runnin', hey, hey,
   Behind the stadium with you,
   My brown eyed girl,
   You, my brown eyed girl.

# Blowin' in the Wind

**Words and Music by Bob Dylan**

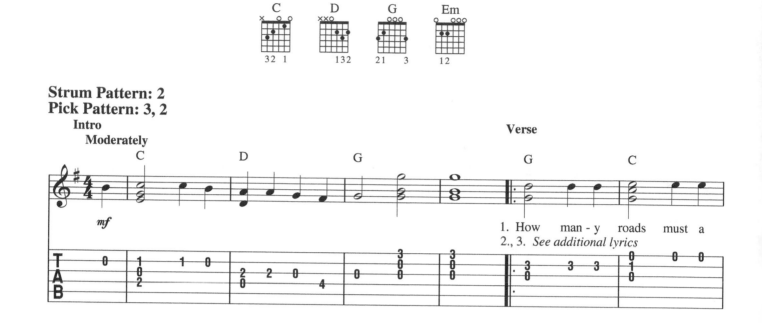

**Strum Pattern: 2**
**Pick Pattern: 3, 2**

Intro
Moderately

Verse

1. How man-y roads must a
2., 3. *See additional lyrics*

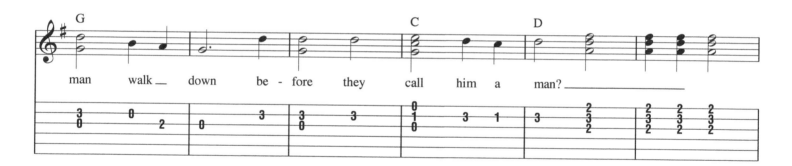

man walk down be-fore they call him a man?

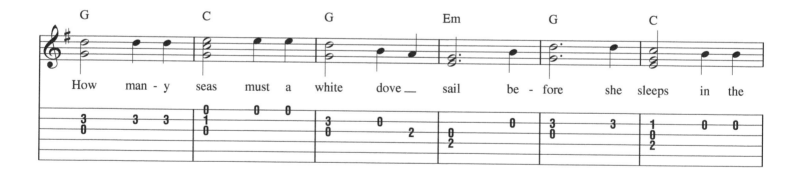

How man-y seas must a white dove sail be-fore she sleeps in the

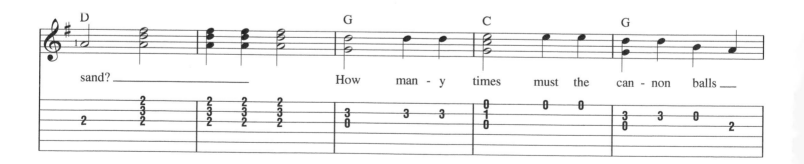

sand? How man-y times must the can-non balls

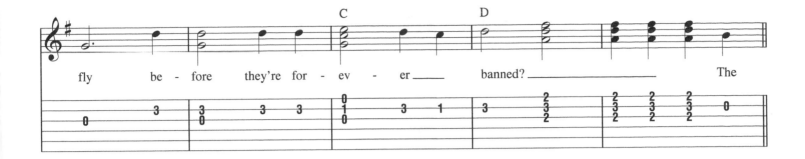

fly be - fore they're for - ev - er ____ banned? _____ The

**Chorus**

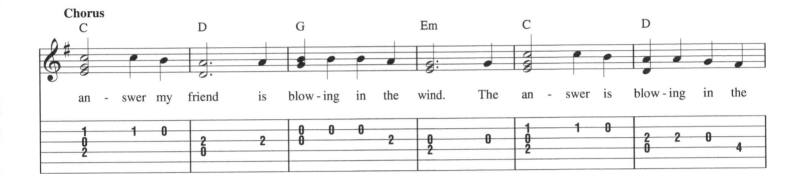

an - swer my friend is blow - ing in the wind. The an - swer is blow - ing in the

wind. ____ wind. ____

**Outro**

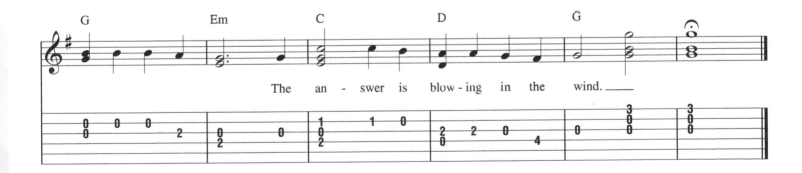

The an - swer is blow - ing in the wind. ____

*Additional Lyrics*

2. How many years must a mountain exist
Before it is washed to the sea?
How many years can some people exist
Before they're allowed to be free?
How many times can a man turn his head
And pretend that he just doesn't see?

3. How many times must a man look up
Before he can see the sky?
How many ears must one man have
Before he can hear people cry?
How many deaths will it take till he knows
That too many people have died?

# Candle in the Wind

**Words and Music by Elton John and Bernie Taupin**

*Capo II

**Strum Pattern: 3**
**Pick Pattern: 2**

Verse
Moderately

1. Good- bye, Nor - ma Jean. ___ Though I nev - er knew you ___ at all, ___
2., 3. *See additional lyrics*

*Optional: To match recording, place capo at 2nd fret.

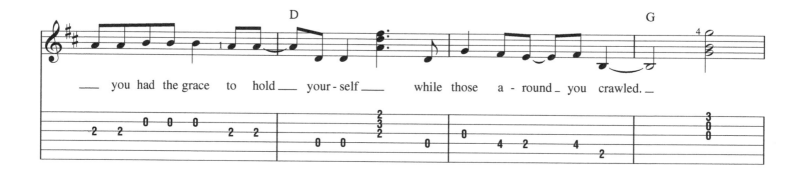

___ you had the grace to hold ___ your - self ___ while those a - round ___ you crawled. ___

They crawled out of the wood-work and they whis-pered in - to ___ your brain. ___

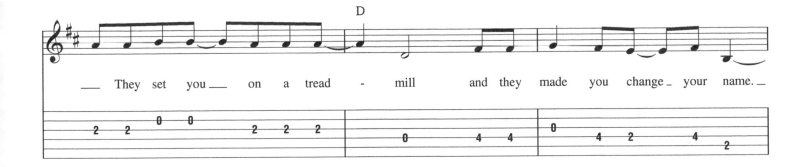

They set you — on a tread - mill and they made you change — your name. —

**Chorus**

And it seems to me — you lived your life — like a

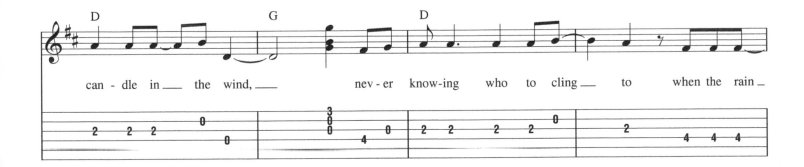

can - dle in — the wind, — nev - er know-ing who to cling — to when the rain —

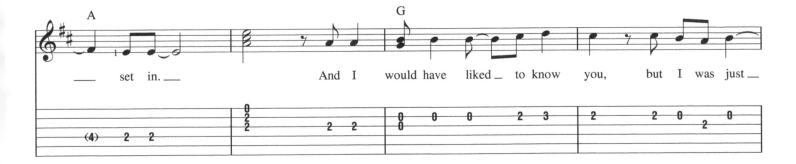

— set in. — And I would have liked — to know you, but I was just —

— a kid. Your can - dle burned _ out long be - fore _ your leg-end ev - er did. _

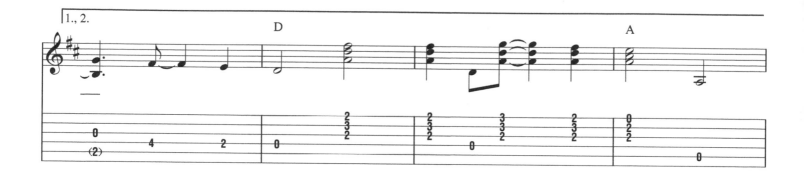

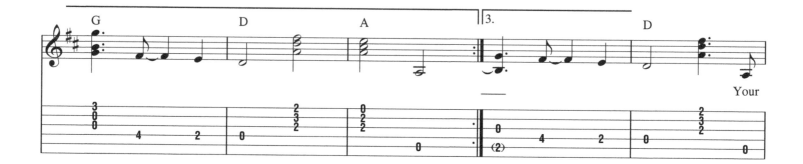

Your

can - dle burned _ out long be - fore _ your leg-end ev - er did. ____

*Additional Lyrics*

2. Loneliness was tough, the toughest role you ever played.
   Hollywood created a superstar and pain was the price you paid.
   And even when you died, oh, the press still hounded you.
   All the papers had to say was that Marilyn was found in the nude.

3. Goodbye, Norma Jean. Though I never knew you at all,
   You had the grace to hold yourself while those around you crawled.
   Goodbye, Norma Jean, from a young man in the twenty-second row,
   Who sees you as something more than sexual, more than just our Marilyn Monroe.

# Fields of Gold

**Music and Lyrics by Sting**

*Capo II
**Strum Pattern: 6**
**Pick Pattern: 4**

**Verse**
**Moderately**

1. You'll re - mem - ber me ___ when the west wind moves ___ up - on the fields ___ of bar -
3. *See additional lyrics*

*Optional: To match recording, place capo at 2nd fret.

- ley.     You'll for - get the sun ___ in his jeal - ous sky ___ as we

**Interlude**

walk in fields ___ of gold.

**Verse**

2. So she took her love ___ for to gaze a - while ___ up - on the fields ___ of bar -
4. *See additional lyrics*

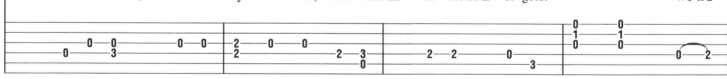

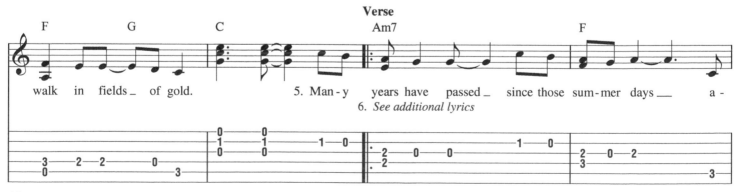

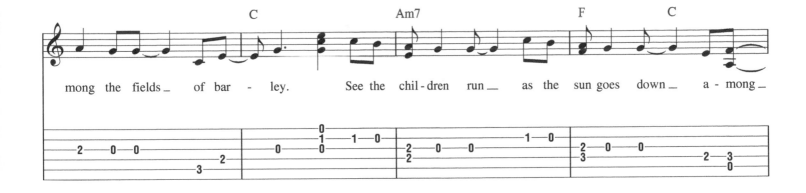

mong the fields _ of bar - ley. See the chil-dren run _ as the sun goes down _ a - mong _

_ the fields _ of gold. 6. You'll re - —— in fields _ of gold, when we

walked in fields _ of gold, when we walked in fields _ of gold.

*Additional Lyrics*

3. Will you stay with me, will you be my love
   Among the fields of barley?
   We'll forget the sun in his jealous sky
   As we lie in fields of gold.

4. See the west wind move like a lover so,
   Upon the fields of barley.
   Feel her body rise when you kiss her mouth
   Among the fields of gold.

6. You'll remember me when the west wind moves
   Upon the fields of barley.
   You can tell the sun in his jealous sky
   When we walked in fields of gold,
   When we walked in fields of gold,
   When we walked in fields of gold.

# Drift Away

Words and Music by Mentor Williams

*Optional: To match recording, place capo at 2nd fret.

1. Day af - ter day, I'm ___ more con - fused, ___ yet I look for the
2. Be - gin - nin' to think that I'm wast - in' time. ___ I don't un - der -
3. Thanks ___ for the joy that you've giv - en me. ___ I want you to know

light through the pour - ing rain. ___ You know that's a game that I hate ___ to lose. ___
stand the things I do. ___ The world out - side looks so ___ un -
___ I be lieve in your song ___ and rhy - thm and rhyme and har - mo - ny.

kind. ___
And I'm feel - in' the strain; ___ ain't it a shame? ___
And I'm count - in' on you. ___ to car - ry me through. ___ } Oh,
You help me a - long ___ mak - in' me strong. ___ }

*To Coda*

**Chorus**

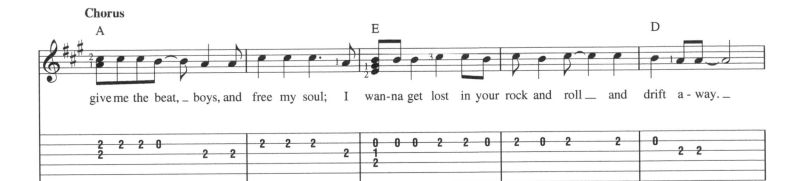

give me the beat, _ boys, and free my soul; I wan-na get lost in your rock and roll _ and drift a - way. _

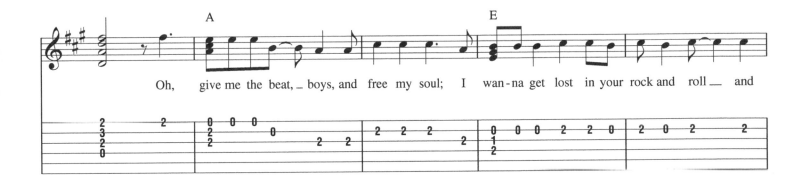

Oh, give me the beat, _ boys, and free my soul; I wan-na get lost in your rock and roll _ and

drift a - way. _

**Bridge**

And when my mind _ is free, _

you know a mel - o - dy can move __ me.    And when I'm feel-

*D.S. al Coda*

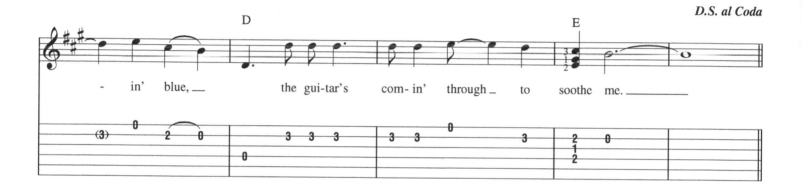

- in' blue, __    the gui-tar's com-in' through __ to    soothe me. _____

**Coda**

**Chorus**

give } me the beat, __ boys, and  free  my  soul.  I  wan - na  get  lost  in  your
Give }

rock and roll __ and  drift a - way. _____                                              Oh, _____

give me the beat,— boys, and free my soul. I wan-na get lost in your

rock and roll — and drift a-way.—　　　　Oh,　　hey, — hey, — yeah,

Now,　now,　now won't ya,　won't ya take me?　　Whoa, ___ take me.

*Lyrics sung 1st time only (next 3 meas.).

*Repeat and fade*

# Every Rose Has Its Thorn

**Words and Music by Bobby Dall, C.C. Deville, Bret Michaels and Rikki Rockett**

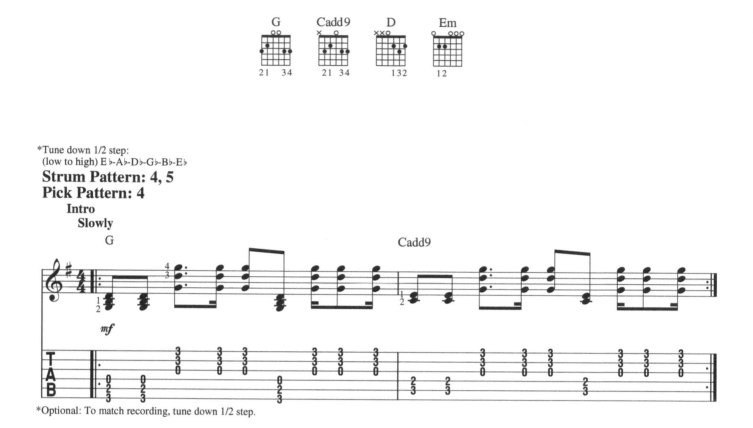

*Tune down 1/2 step:
(low to high) E♭-A♭-D♭-G♭-B♭-E♭

**Strum Pattern: 4, 5**
**Pick Pattern: 4**

Intro
Slowly

*Optional: To match recording, tune down 1/2 step.

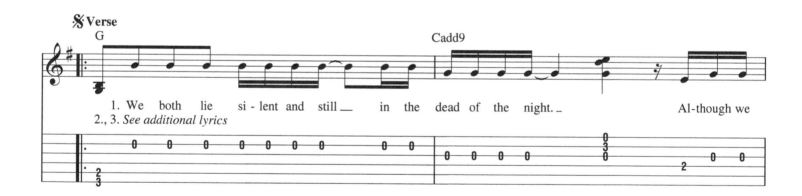

Verse

1. We both lie si-lent and still ___ in the dead of the night. ___  Al-though we

2., 3. *See additional lyrics*

both lie close to-geth - er,  we feel miles a-part ___ in - side. ___  Was it

some-thin' I said or some-thin' I did? Did my words not come out right? Though I

tried not to hurt ___ you, though I tried. But I guess that's why they say

**Chorus**

ev - 'ry rose ___ has its thorn, just like ev - 'ry night ___ has its dawn. _____ Just like

*To Coda* ⊕ |1.

ev - 'ry cow - boy sings a sad, sad ___ song, ev - 'ry rose has its thorn. _ *Spoken: Yeah, it does.*

*Let chord ring.

**Interlude**

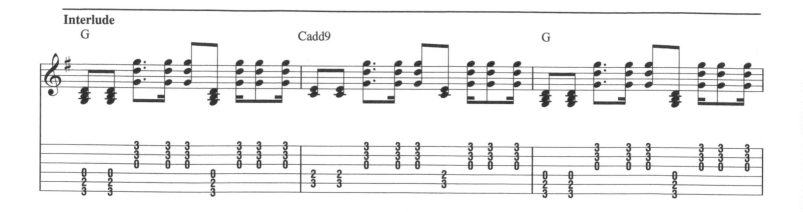

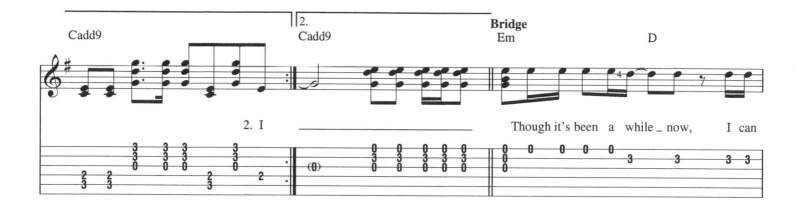

2. I _____ Though it's been a while \_ now, I can

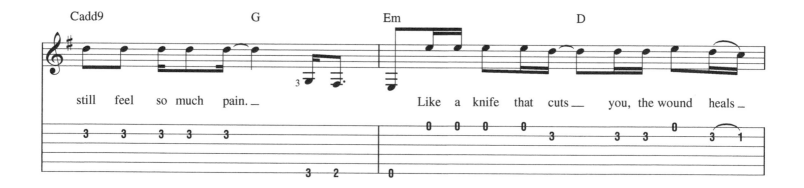

still feel so much pain. \_ Like a knife that cuts \_ you, the wound heals \_

**Guitar Solo**

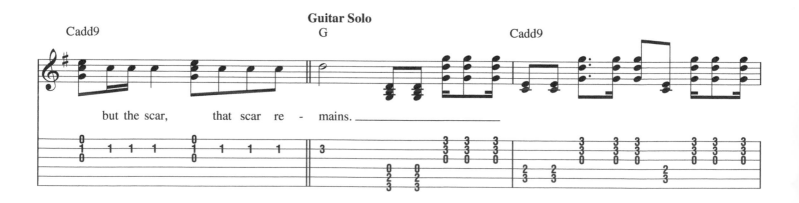

but the scar, that scar re - mains. _____

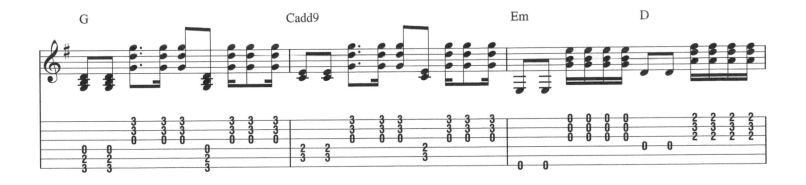

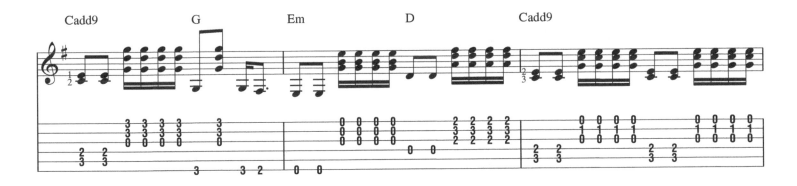

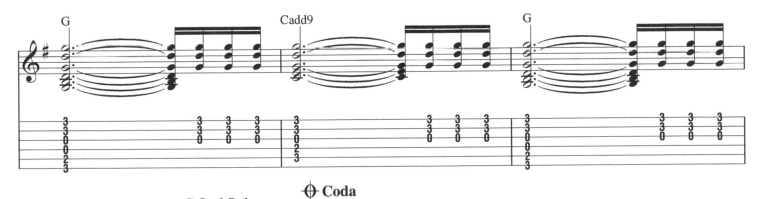

**D.S. al Coda**

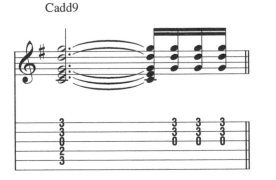

**Coda**

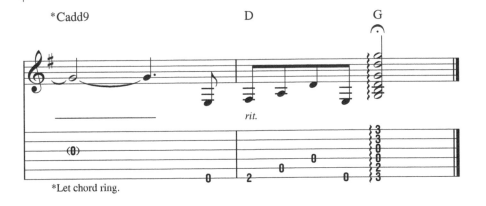

*Let chord ring.

---

*Additional Lyrics*

2. I listen to our fav'rite song playin' on the radio.
   Hear the DJ say love's a game of easy come and easy go.
   But I wonder, does he know? Has he ever felt like this?
   And I know that you'd be here right now if I could-a let you know somehow.
   I guess...

3. I know I could-a saved a love that night if I'd known what to say.
   'Stead of makin' love, we both made our sep'rate ways.
   And now I hear you found somebody new and that I never meant that much to you.
   To hear that tears me up inside, and to see you cuts me like a knife.
   I guess...

# Have You Ever Seen the Rain?

**Words and Music by John Fogerty**

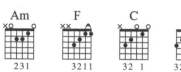

**Strum Pattern: 1**
**Pick Pattern: 5**

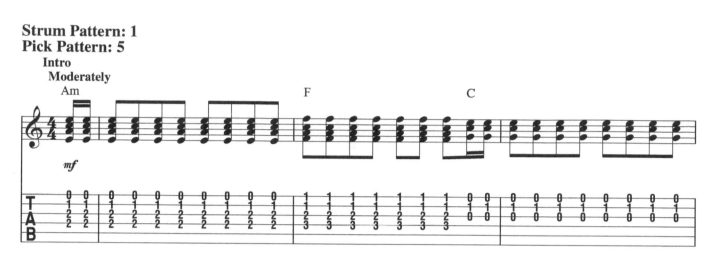

1. Some-one told me long
2. Yes - ter-day and days

— a - go, — there's a calm be - fore — the storm. I know, —
— be - fore, — sun is cold and rain — is hard. — I know, —

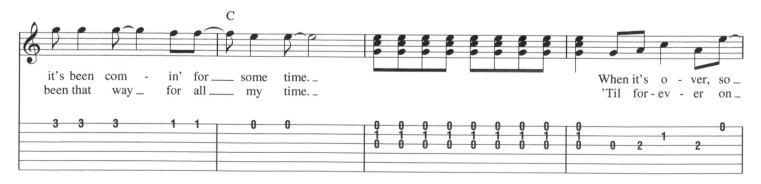

it's been com - in' for — some time. — When it's o - ver, so —
been that way — for all — my time. — 'Til for - ev - er on —

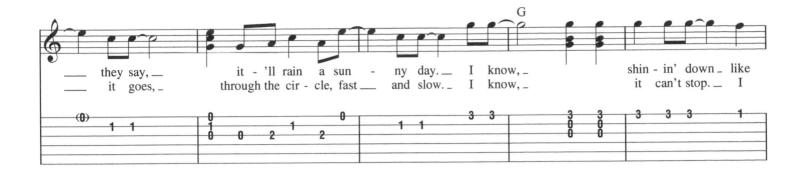

_____ they say, _____ it -'ll rain a sun - ny day. _ I know, _ shin - in' down _ like
_____ it goes, _____ through the cir - cle, fast _ and slow. _ I know, _ it can't stop. _ I

%. **Chorus**

wa - ter. }
won - der. }
I want to know, _ have you ev - er seen the

_To Coda_ 1.

rain? I want to know, _ have you ev - er seen the rain com - in'

2.

down a sun - ny day? _ com - in' down a sun - ny day? _

**Coda**

_D.S. al Coda_

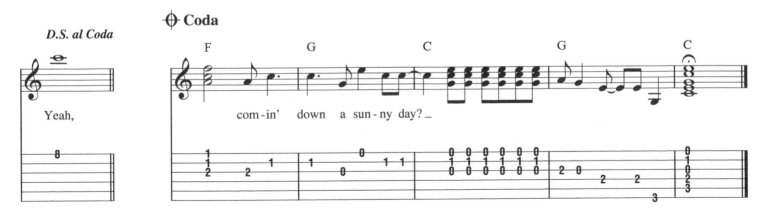

Yeah, com - in' down a sun - ny day? _

# I Saw Her Standing There

Words and Music by John Lennon and Paul McCartney

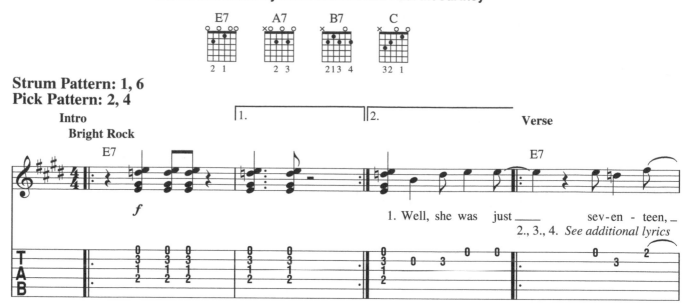

**Strum Pattern: 1, 6**
**Pick Pattern: 2, 4**

1. Well, she was just____ sev-en - teen,____
2., 3., 4. *See additional lyrics*

—— and you know what I mean, __ and the way she looked __ was way __

—— be-yond com - pare. __ So how could I dance __

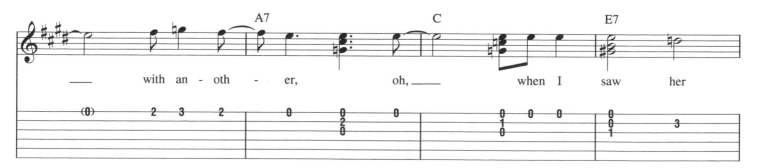

—— with an - oth - er, oh, ____ when I saw her

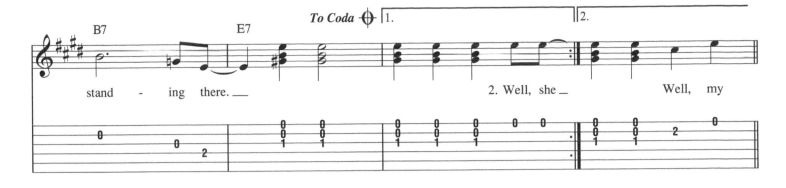

stand - ing there. ___ 2. Well, she ___ Well, my

heart went boom ___ when I crossed that room, ___ and I held her hand ___

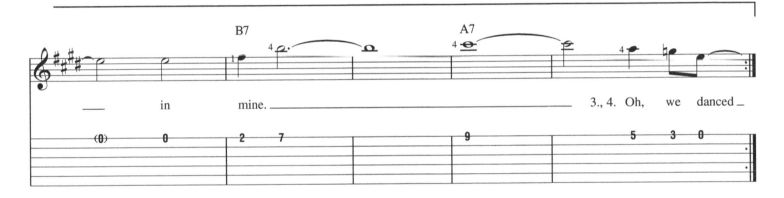

___ in mine. _____ 3., 4. Oh, we danced ___

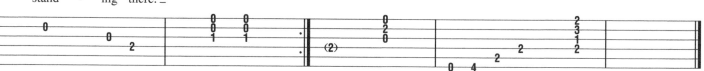

*Additional Lyrics*

2. Well, she looked at me
And I, I could see
That before too long
I'd fall in love with her.
She wouldn't dance with another, whoa,
When I saw her standing there.

3., 4. Oh, we danced through the night
And we held each other tight,
And before too long
I fell in love with her.
Now I'll never dance with another, whoa,
Since I saw her standing there.

# I'm a Believer

**Words and Music by Neil Diamond**

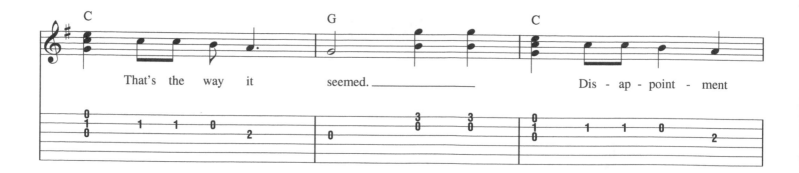

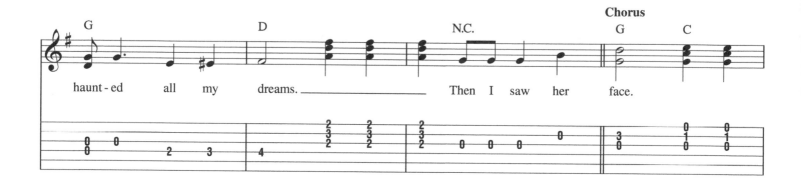

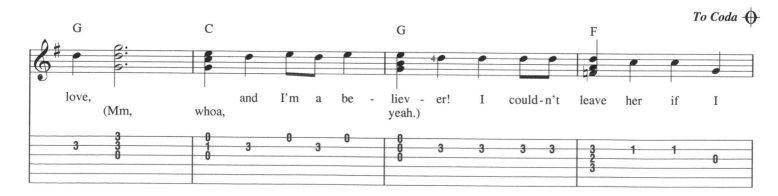

**Guitar Solo**

*D.S. al Coda*

**Coda**

*Additional Lyrics*

2. I thought love was more or less a givin' thing.
   Seems the more I gave, the less I got.
   What's the use in tryin'?
   All you get is pain.
   When I needed sunshine, I got rain.

# I Shot the Sheriff

**Words and Music by Bob Marley**

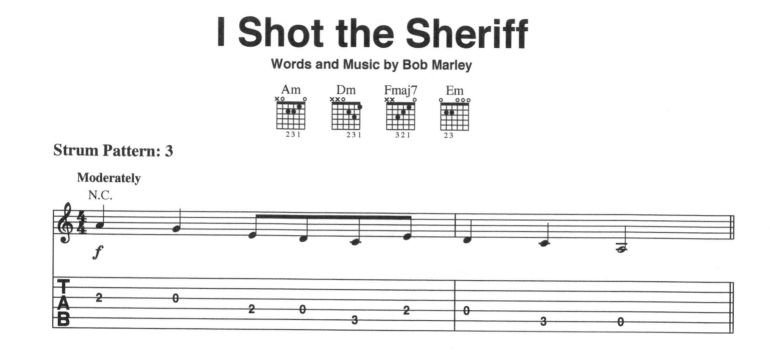

**Strum Pattern: 3**

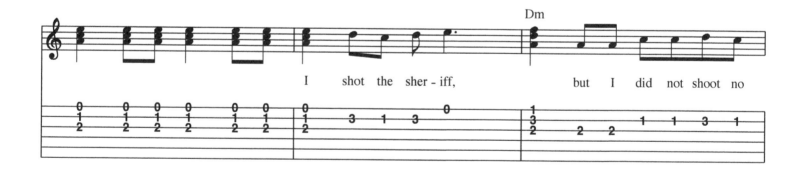

**Additional Lyrics**

2. Sheriff John Brown always hated me;
   For what, I don't know.
   And every time that I plant a seed,
   He said, "Kill it before it grows,"
   "Kill it before it grows."

3. Freedom came our way one day,
   So I started out of town.
   All of a sudden, I see Sheriff Brown
   Aimin' to shoot me down,
   So I shot him down.

4. Reflexes got the better of me,
   What will be will be.
   Every day, the bucket goes to the well,
   One day the bottom will drop out
   I say, one day the bottom will drop out.

# Jessie's Girl

**Words and Music by Rick Springfield**

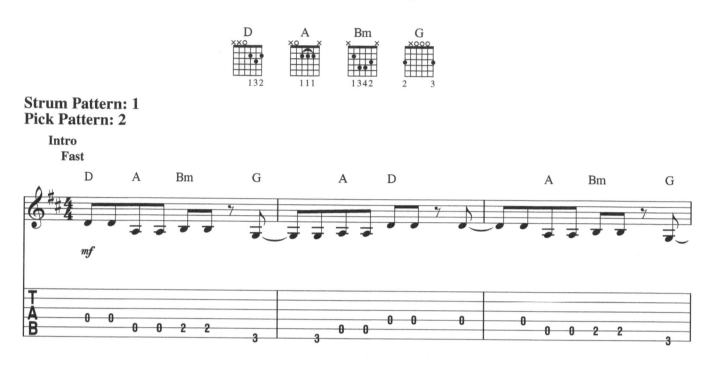

**Strum Pattern: 1**
**Pick Pattern: 2**

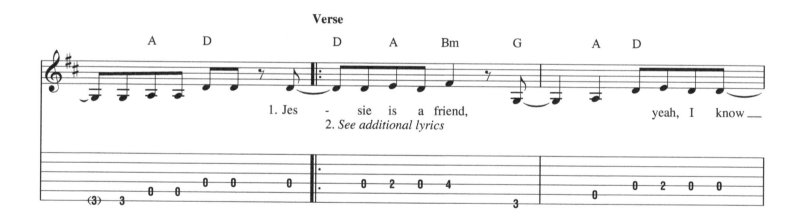

1. Jes - sie is a friend,
2. *See additional lyrics*

yeah, I know ___ ___ he's been a good friend of mine. ___ But late - ly some - thing's changed; ___ it ain't hard ___

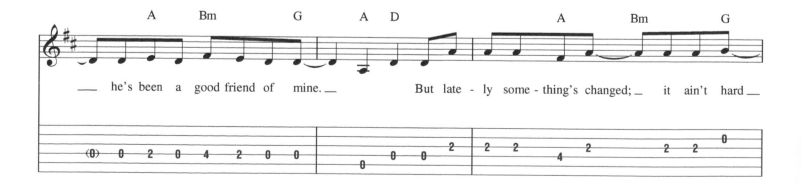

to de-fine.___ Jes-sie's got him-self a girl,___ and I wan-na make her mine.___ And she's / 'Cause she's

**Pre-Chorus**

watch-in' him with those eyes.___ And she's lov-in' him with that___ bod-y. I

just know it! And he's hold ___ in' her in his arms___ late, late at night.___

**Chorus**

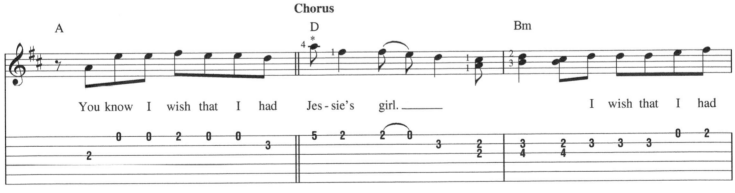

You know I wish that I had Jes-sie's girl._____ I wish that I had

*2nd position.

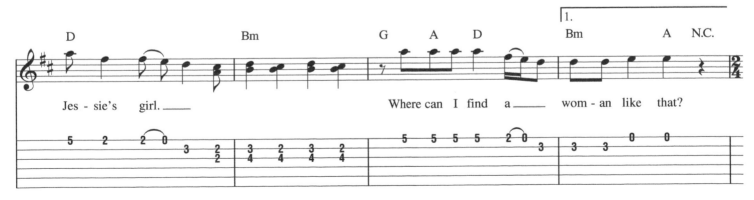

Jes-sie's girl.___ Where can I find a___ wom-an like that?

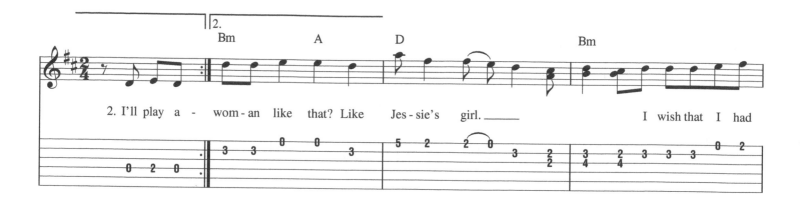

2. I'll play a - wom - an like that? Like Jes - sie's girl.____ I wish that I had

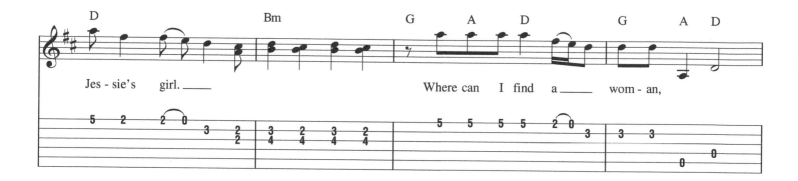

Jes - sie's girl.____ Where can I find a____ wom - an,

**Bridge**

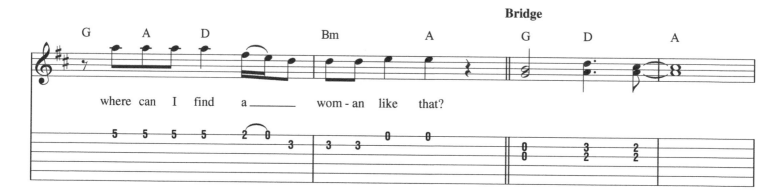

where can I find a____ wom - an like that?

And I look in the mir - or all the time____

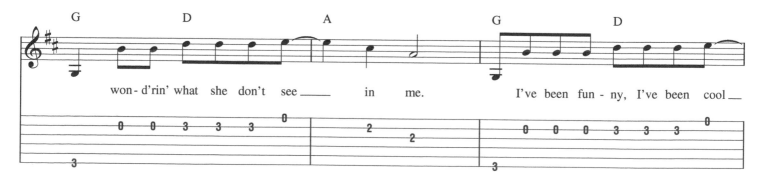

won - d'rin' what she don't see ____ in me. I've been fun - ny, I've been cool ____

with the lines. ___ Ain't that the way love's sup - posed ___ to be?

**Interlude**

Tell me

**Guitar Solo**

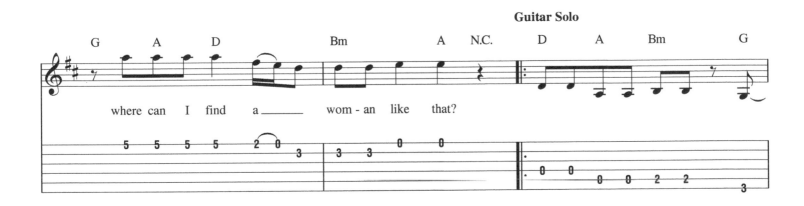

where can I find a ___ wom - an like that?

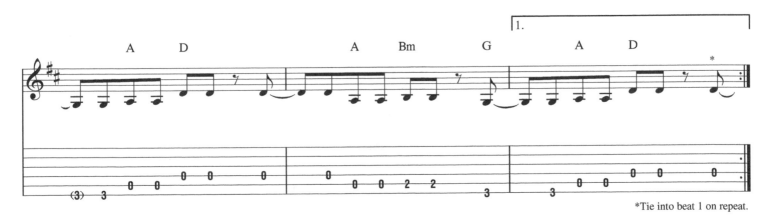

*Tie into beat 1 on repeat.

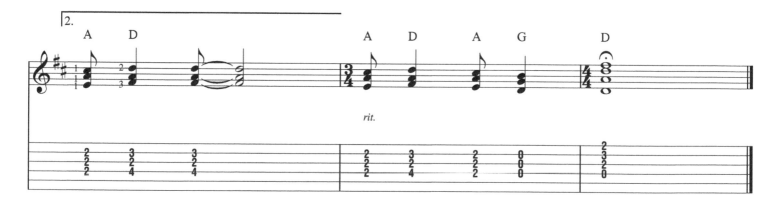

*Additional Lyrics*

2. I'll play along with this charade.
There doesn't seem to be a reason to change.
You know, I feel so dirty when they start talkin' cute.
I wanna tell her that I love her, but the point is prob'ly moot.

# No Woman No Cry

**Words and Music by Vincent Ford**

*Organ arr. for gtr., next 4 1/2 meas.

**Chorus**

No,
no, } wom-an, no cry. ___

No, wom-an, no cry. ___

{ No, wom-an, no cry.
Here, ___ lit-tle dar-lin', don't shed no tears. }

No, wom-an, no cry. ___

**Verse**

Said, said.

1. Said, I re-mem-ber when we used ___ to sit

2., 3. *See additional lyrics*

wom- an, no wom- an, no cry. ___      Oh, my lit- tle sis- ter,      don't shed no tears. _

**Guitar Solo**

No, wom- an, no cry. ___

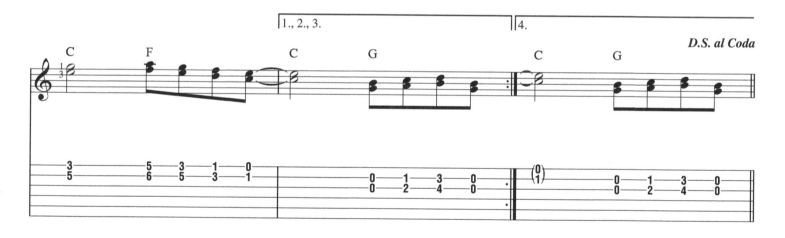

1., 2., 3.      4.

*D.S. al Coda*

**Coda**

**Chorus**

___ through,      but while I'm gone, I mean...      No, wom- an, no cry. ___

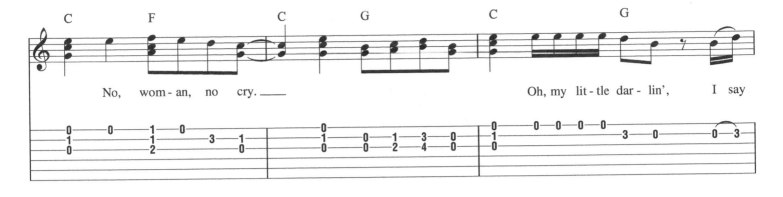

No, wom-an, no cry. ___      Oh, my lit-tle dar-lin',    I say

don't shed no tears. ___     No, wom-an, no cry. ___      Yeah.

**Outro**

Lit-tle {dar-lin',/sis-ter,}    don't shed no tears. ___     No, wom-an, no cry. ___

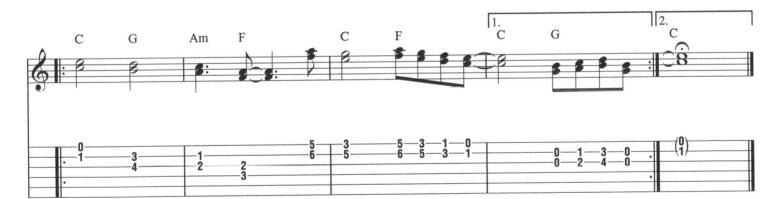

*Additional Lyrics*

2., 3.   Said I remember when we used to sit
In the government's yard in Trenchtown.
And then Georgie would make a firelight
As it was logwood burnin' through the night.
Then we would cook corn meal porridge
Of which I'll share with you.
My feet is my only carriage,
So, I've got to push on through, but while I'm gone I mean...

# Last Kiss

**Words and Music by Wayne Cochran**

**Strum Pattern: 6**
**Pick Pattern: 4**

**Chorus**
Moderately

Oh, where, oh, where can my ___ ba-by be? The Lord took her a-way from me. ___

She's gone to heav-en so I got to be good ___ so I can see my ba-by when I leave _____ this

**Verse**

world. 1. We were out on a date in my ___ dad-dy's car,

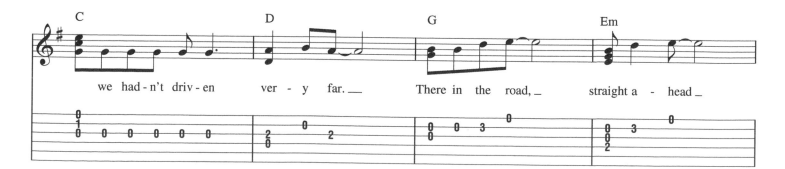

we had-n't driv-en ver-y far. ___ There in the road, ___ straight a-head ___

a car was — stalled, the en-gine was dead. — I could-n't stop — so I swerved to the right. — I'll

nev-er for-get — the sound that night. — The scream-in' tires, — the bust-in' glass, — the

**𝄋 Chorus**

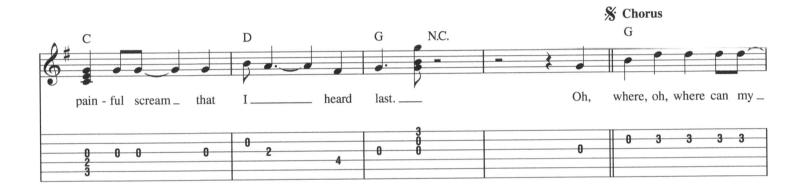

pain-ful scream — that I _____ heard last. _____ Oh, where, oh, where can my —

— ba-by be? The Lord took her a-way from me. _____ She's gone to heav-en so I

*To Coda* ⊕

got to be good _____ so I can see my ba-by when I leave _____ this world.

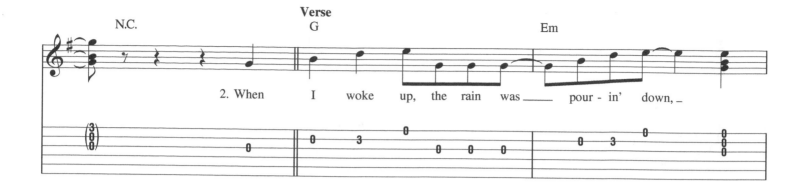

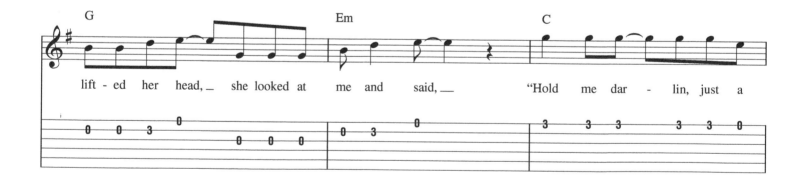

knew I had missed. __ Well, now she's gone __ e - ven though I hold her tight. I

*D.S. al Coda*

lost my love, __ my life _____ that night. Oh,

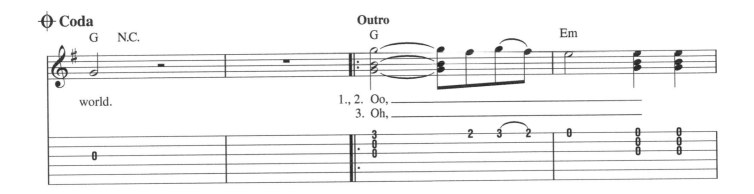

**Coda**    **Outro**

world.

1., 2. Oo, _____
3. Oh, _____

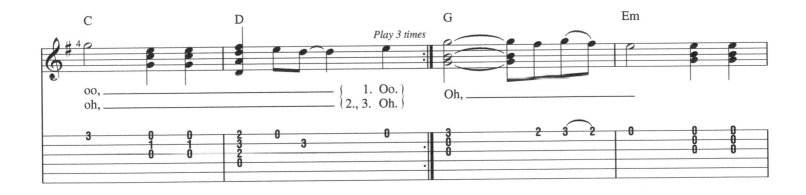

oo, _____
oh, _____

{ 1. Oo. }
{ 2., 3. Oh. }

Oh, _____

*Play 3 times*

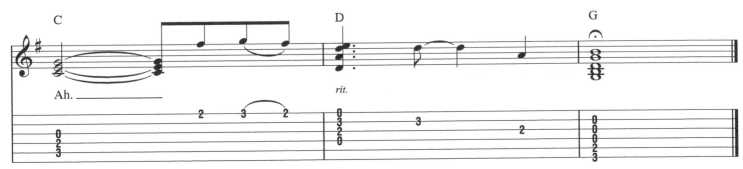

Ah. _____    *rit.*

# Learning to Fly

**Words and Music by Tom Petty and Jeff Lynne**

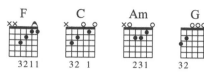

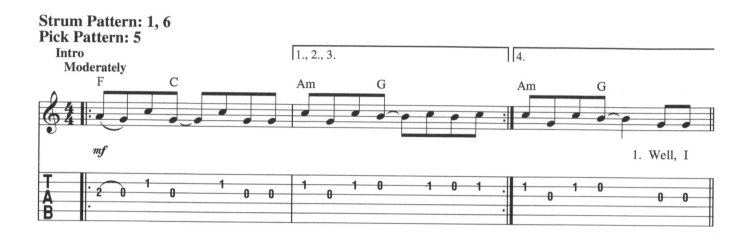

**Strum Pattern: 1, 6**
**Pick Pattern: 5**

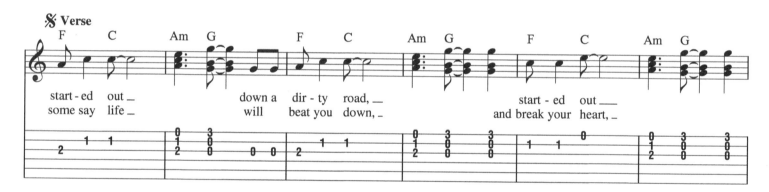

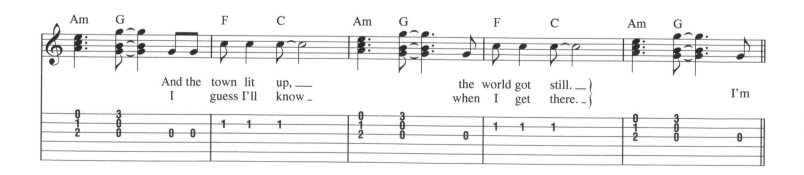

learn-ing to fly — { but I ain't got wings. —
a - round the clouds. —

Com-ing down —
What goes up —

*To Coda* ⊕                    **Verse**

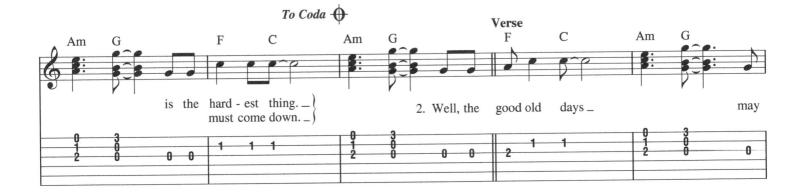

is the hard - est thing. —}
must come down. —}

2. Well, the good old days — may

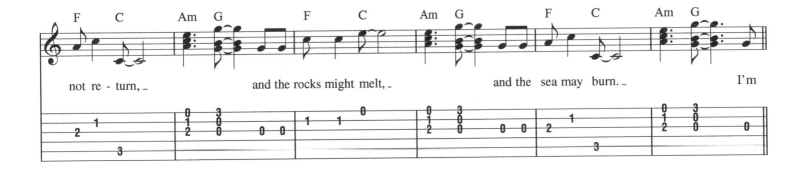

not re - turn, —        and the rocks might melt, —        and the sea may burn. —        I'm

**Chorus**

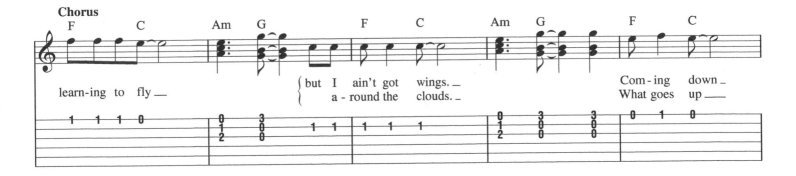

learn-ing to fly — { but I ain't got wings. —
a - round the clouds. —

Com-ing down —
What goes up —

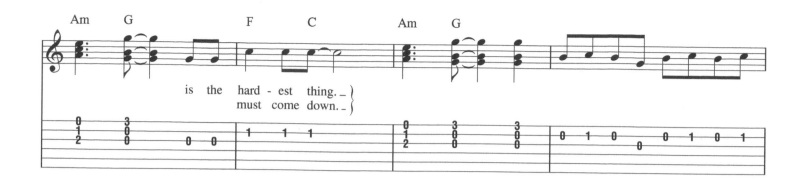

is the hard-est thing. ⟩
must come down. ⟩

**Guitar Solo**

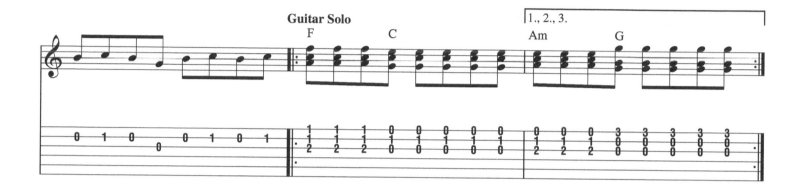

|1., 2., 3.

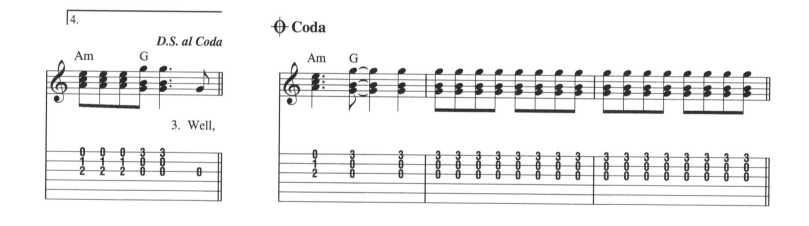

|4.

***D.S. al Coda***

3. Well,

⊕ **Coda**

**Interlude**

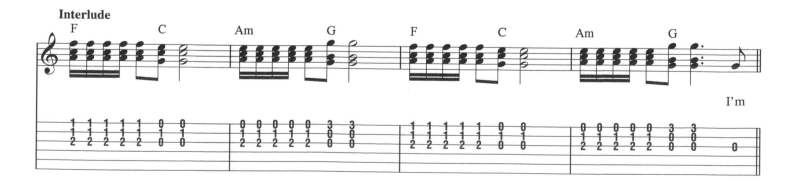

I'm

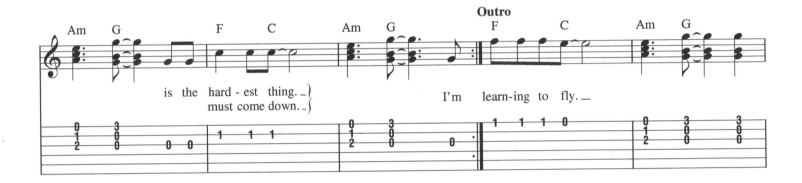

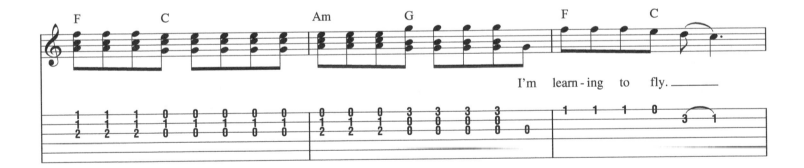

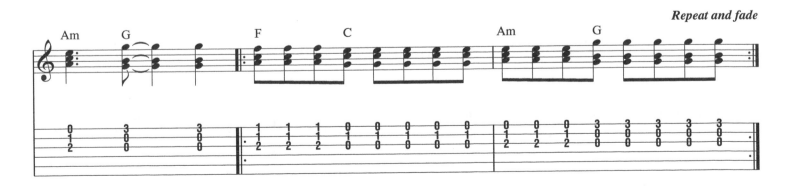

# Pink Houses

**Words and Music by John Mellencamp**

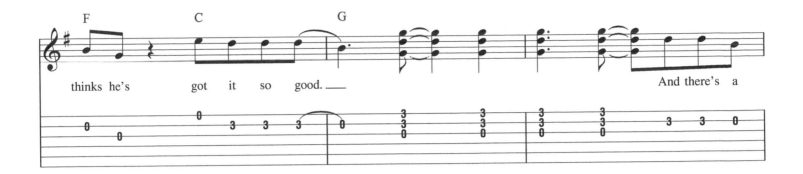

thinks he's got it so good. ____ And there's a

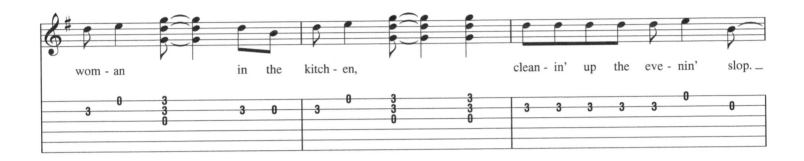

wom-an in the kitch-en, clean-in' up the eve-nin' slop. ____

____ And he looks at her and says, "Hey Dar-lin,' I can r'mem-ber when you could

**Chorus**

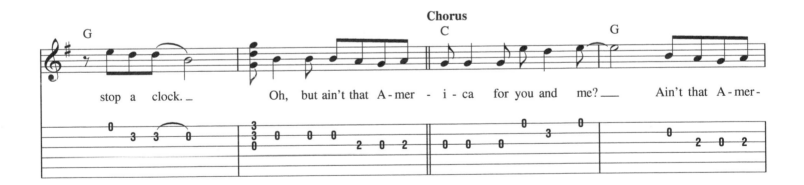

stop a clock. _ Oh, but ain't that A-mer-i-ca for you and me? ____ Ain't that A-mer-

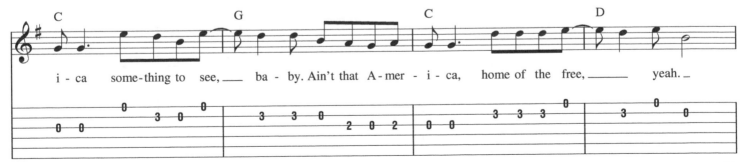

i-ca some-thing to see, ____ ba-by. Ain't that A-mer-i-ca, home of the free, ____ yeah. ____

*To Coda* ⊕

Lit - tle pink hous - es for you and me.

2. Well, there's a

**Guitar Solo**

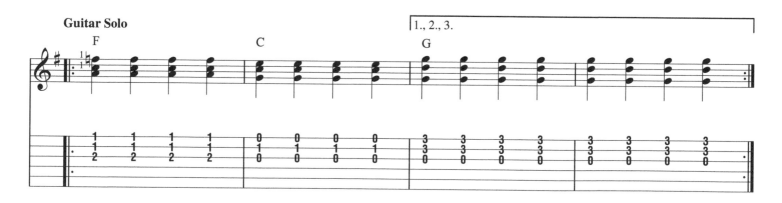

*D.S. al Coda*

3. Well, there's peo -

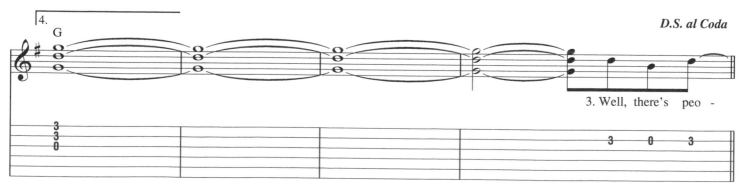

**Outro-Chorus**

Ain't that A-mer - i - ca for you and me? _

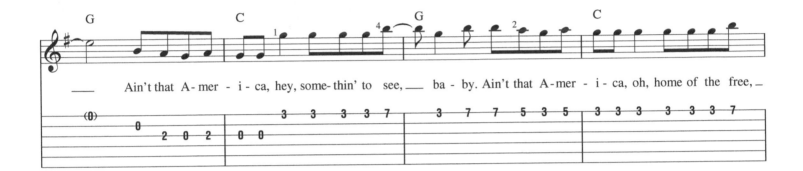

_ Ain't that A-mer - i - ca, hey, some-thin' to see, _ ba - by. Ain't that A-mer - i - ca, oh, home of the free, _

_ yeah, yeah, yeah, yeah, yeah, yeah, yeah. Lit-tle pink hous - es for you and me. _

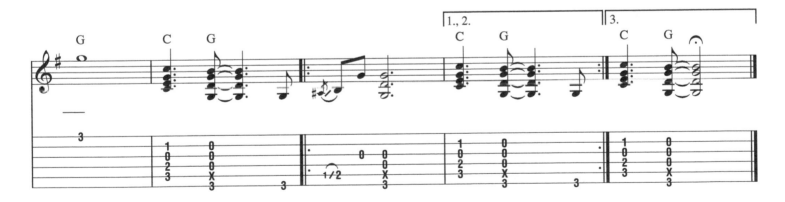

*Additional Lyrics*

2. Well, there's a young man in a tee shirt.
   He's list'nin' to a rock 'n' roller station.
   He's got a greasy hair and greasy smile.
   He says, "Lord, this must be my destination."
   'Cause they told me when I was younger,
   They said, "Boy, you're gonna be president."
   But just like ev'rything else,
   Those old crazy dreams kind of came and went.

3. Well, there's people and more people.
   What do they know, know, know?
   Go to work in some high-rise
   And vacation down at the Gulf of Mexico.
   And there's winners and there's losers,
   But they ain't no big deal.
   'Cause the simple man, baby,
   Pays for thrills, the bills and pills that kill.

# Should I Stay or Should I Go

### Words and Music by Mick Jones and Joe Strummer

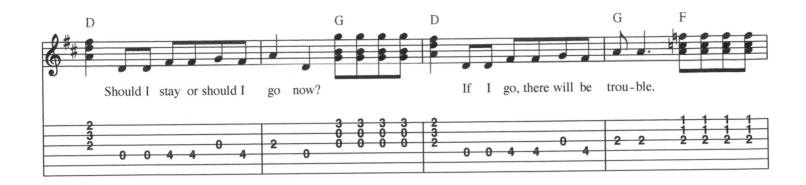

Should I stay or should I go now? If I go, there will be trou-ble.

*To Coda* ⊕

And if I stay, it will be dou-ble. So you've got to let me know: —

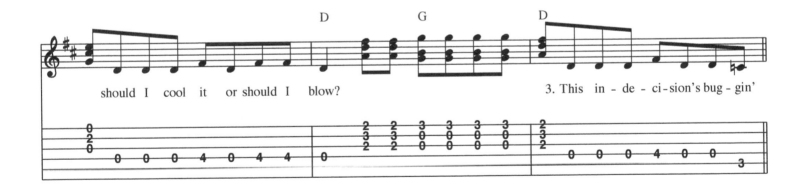

should I cool it or should I blow? 3. This in-de-ci-sion's bug-gin'

**Verse**

me. If you don't want me set me free. Ex-act-ly who'm I s'posed to

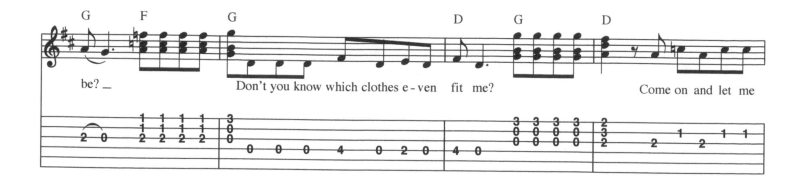

be? ___ Don't you know which clothes e - ven fit me? Come on and let me

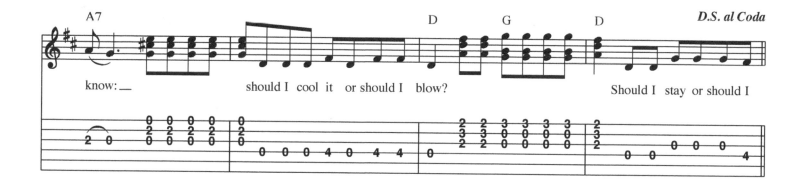

*D.S. al Coda*

know: ___ should I cool it or should I blow? Should I stay or should I

✛ **Coda**

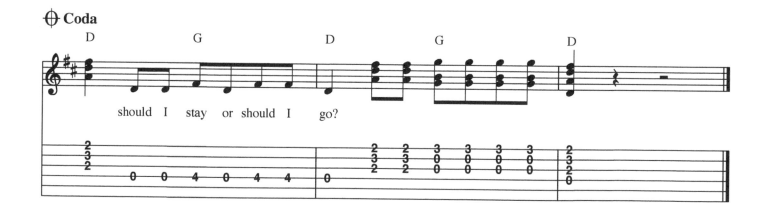

should I stay or should I go?

*Additional Lyrics*

2. It's always tease, tease, tease.
   You're happy when I'm on my knees.
   One day is fine and next is black.
   So if you want me off your back,
   Well, come on and let me know:
   Should I stay or should I go?

# Stuck in the Middle with You

**Words and Music by Gerry Rafferty and Joe Egan**

**Strum Pattern: 1**
**Pick Pattern: 2, 5**

Intro
Moderately

1., 5. Well, I don't —

Verse

____ know why I came here to - night. ____ I got the feel - in' that some - thing ain't right. ____
____ stuck in the mid - dle with you, ____ and I'm won - d'ring what it is I should do. ____
3. Try'n' to make some sense of it all, ____ but I can see ____ it makes no ____ sense at all.
4. *Instrumental*

____ I'm so scared ____ in case I fall off my chair ____ and I'm won -
It's so hard ____ to keep this smile from my face. ____ Los - ing con -
Is it cool ____ to go to sleep on the floor? ____ You don't think ____

d'ring how I'll get down the stairs. ___
trol and I'm all o - ver the place. ___
___ that I can take an - y - more. ___

Clowns ___ to the left of me, jok -

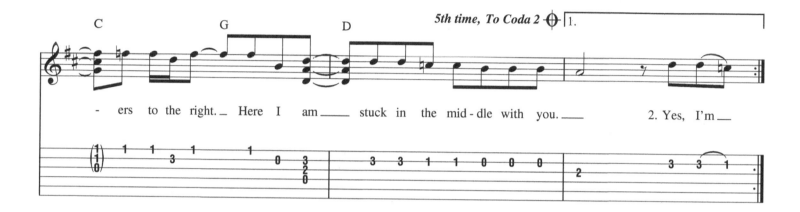

**5th time, To Coda 2** ⊕ 1.

- ers to the right. __ Here I am __ stuck in the mid - dle with you. __   2. Yes, I'm __

2.

**Bridge**

G

*Instrumental ends* } Well, you start - ed out with noth - in', and you're proud that you're a self - made man.

D                                                                    G

And your friends, they all come call - in', slap __

you on the back and say, "Please, ____

*To Coda 1* ⊕      *D.S. al Coda 1*        ⊕ **Coda 1**        *D.S. al Coda 2*
*(take repeat)*

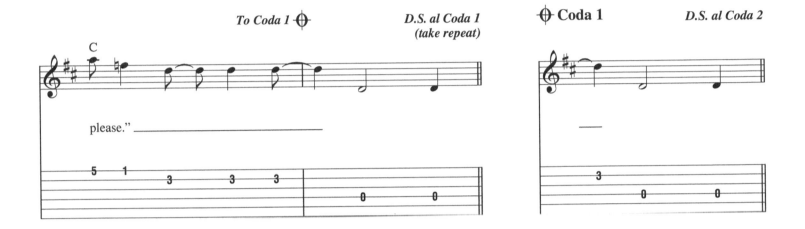

please." ____

⊕ **Coda 2**

____ Yes, I'm stuck in the mid-dle with you. ____ stuck in the mid-dle with you. ____

____ Here I am, ____ stuck in the mid-dle with you. ____

# Surfin' Safari

**Words and Music by Brian Wilson and Mike Love**

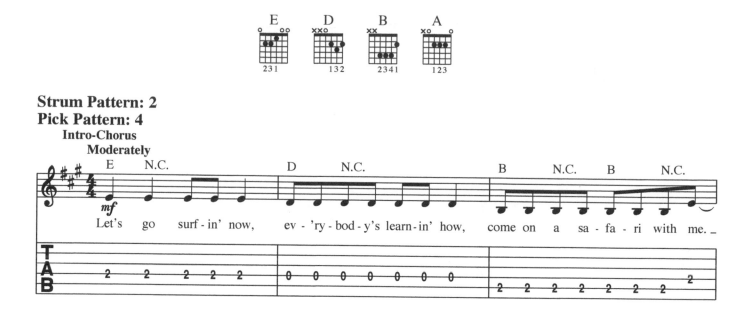

**Strum Pattern: 2**
**Pick Pattern: 4**

Intro-Chorus
Moderately

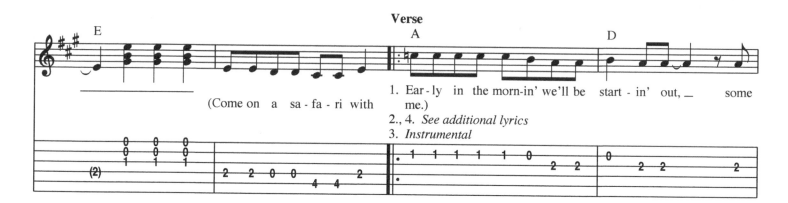

Let's go surf-in' now, ev-'ry-bod-y's learn-in' how, come on a sa-fa-ri with me. _

**Verse**

(Come on a sa-fa-ri with me.)

1. Ear-ly in the morn-in' we'll be start-in' out, _ some
2., 4. *See additional lyrics*
3. *Instrumental*

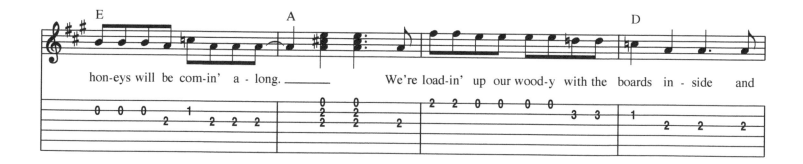

hon-eys will be com-in' a-long. _____ We're load-in' up our wood-y with the boards in-side and

**Chorus**

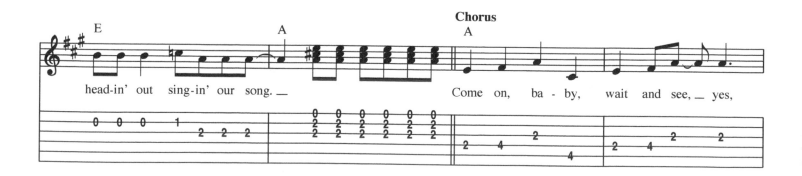

head-in' out sing-in' our song. _ Come on, ba-by, wait and see, _ yes,

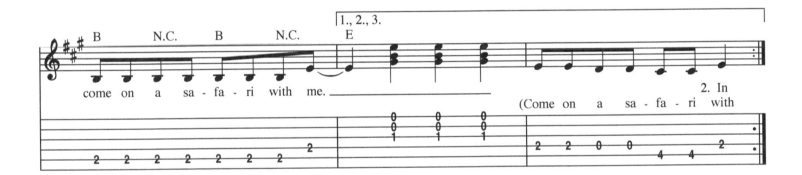

*Additional Lyrics*

2. In Huntington and Malibu they're shootin' the pier,
   In Rincon, they're walkin' the nose.
   We're goin' on safari to the islands this year,
   So if you're comin', get ready to go.

4. They're anglin' in Laguna and Cerro Azul,
   They're kickin' out in Dohini too.
   I'll tell you surfin's runnin' wild, it's gettin' bigger ev'ry day
   From Hawaii to the shores of Peru.

# Teach Your Children

**Words and Music by Graham Nash**

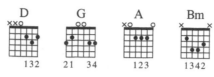

**Strum Pattern: 3, 4**
**Pick Pattern: 1, 3**

**Intro**
Moderately slow, in 2

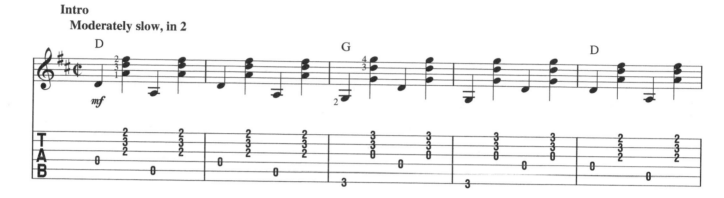

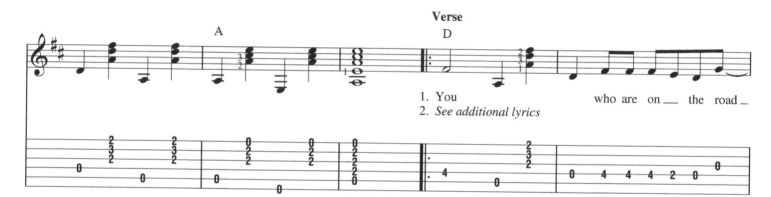

1. You who are on __ the road __
2. *See additional lyrics*

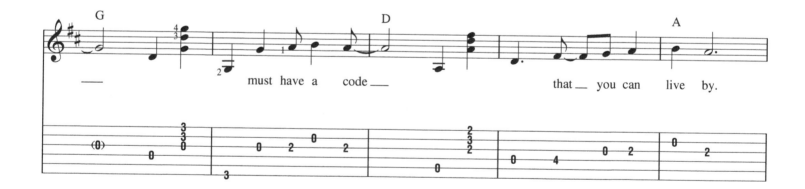

— must have a code __ that __ you can live by.

And so be - come __ your - self be - cause the past __

is just a good - bye. Teach

your {chil - dren / par - ents} well. Their {fa - ther's / chil - dren's} hell

{did / will} slow - ly go —— by. And feed them on —— your

dreams. The one they pick's the one —— you'll

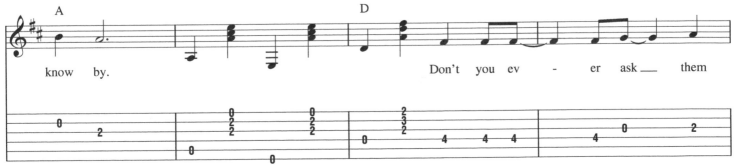

know by. Don't you ev - er ask —— them

why. If they told you, you ___ would cry. _____ So just look at them ___ and

sigh _____ and know they love _____ you.

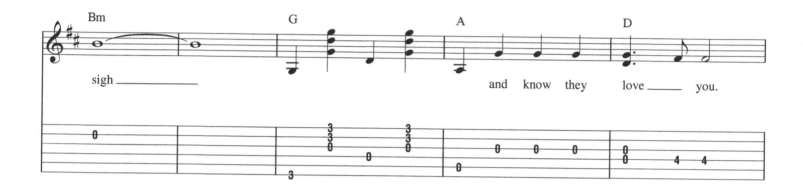

1.

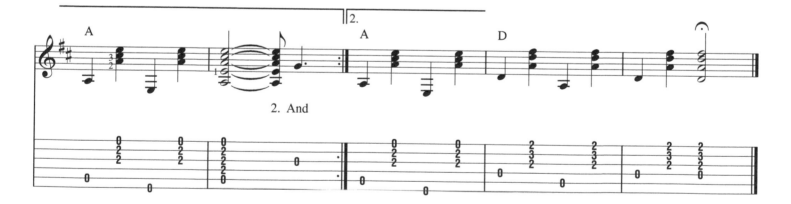

2.

2. And

*Additional Lyrics*

2. And you of the tender years
   Can't know the fears that your elders grew by.
   And so, please help them with your youth.
   They seek the truth before they can die.

# Wanted Dead or Alive

**Words and Music by Jon Bon Jovi and Richie Sambora**

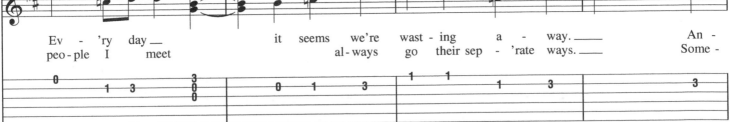

**Strum Pattern: 1, 3**
**Pick Pattern: 2, 4**

Intro
Moderately slow Rock, in 2

*Mute 2nd string w/ back of 2nd finger.

Play 3 times

Verse

3. *Instrumental*
4. *See additional lyrics*

all the same, __ on-ly the names __ will change. __
times I sleep, some-times it's not __ for days. __ The

Ev-'ry day __ it seems we're wast-ing a - way. __ An-
peo-ple I meet al-ways go their sep-'rate ways. __ Some-

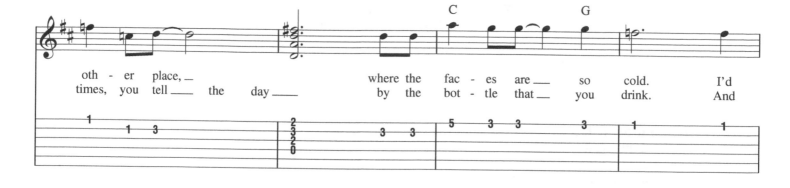

oth - er place, ___ where the fac - es are ___ so cold. I'd
times, you tell ___ the day ___ by the bot - tle that ___ you drink. And

*To Coda 1*

drive all night ___ just to get back ___ home. ___
times when you're a - lone, ___ all you do ___ is think. ___ I'm a

*Instrumental ends*

**Chorus**

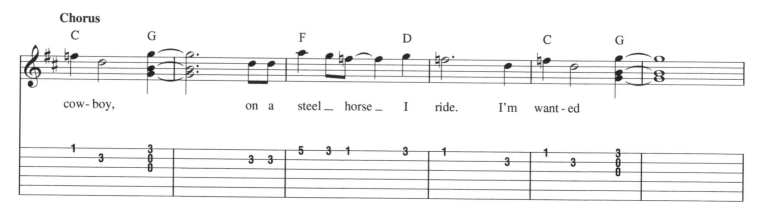

cow- boy, on a steel ___ horse ___ I ride. I'm want - ed

*To Coda 2*

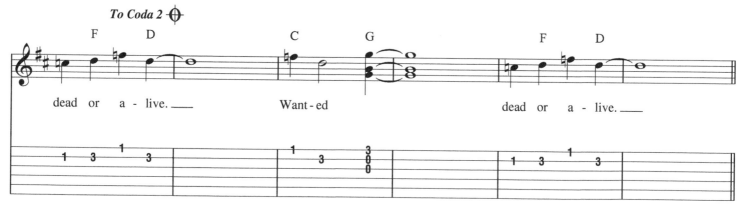

dead or a - live. ___ Want - ed dead or a - live. ___

**Interlude**

N.C.

*Additional Lyrics*

4. And I walk these streets,
   A loaded six-string on my back.
   I've seen a million faces, and I've rocked them all.
   I've been ev'rywhere, still I'm standing tall.
   I play for keeps, 'cause I might not make it back.
   'Cause I'm a...

# Turn the Page

**Words and Music by Bob Seger**

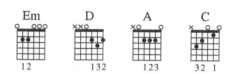

**Strum Pattern: 4**
**Pick Pattern: 5**

Moderately slow

1. On a

**Verse**

long and lone-some high-way, _____ east of O-ma-ha, _____ you can
3. *See additional lyrics*

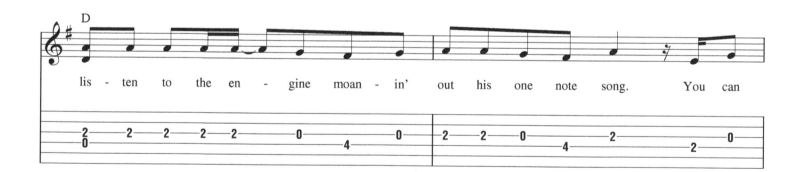

lis-ten to the en-gine moan-in' out his one note song. You can

think a-bout _ the wom-an, _ or the girl you knew the night _ be-fore. _

2. But your thoughts will soon be wan - der - ing, ___ the way they al - ways do, ___ when you're
4., 5. *See additional lyrics*

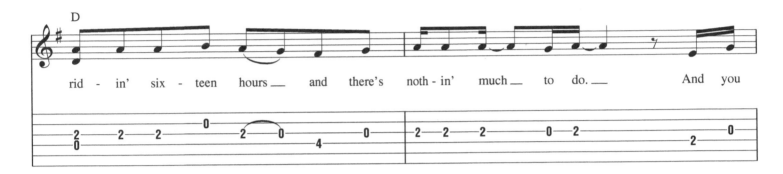

rid - in' six - teen hours ___ and there's noth - in' much ___ to do. ___ And you

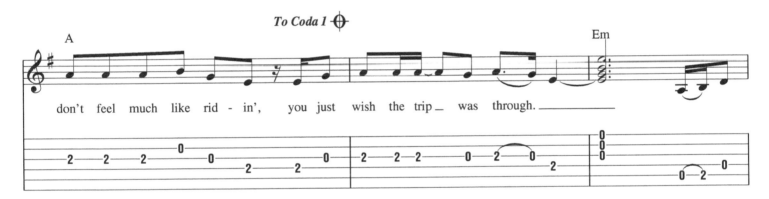

don't feel much like rid - in', you just wish the trip ___ was through. _____

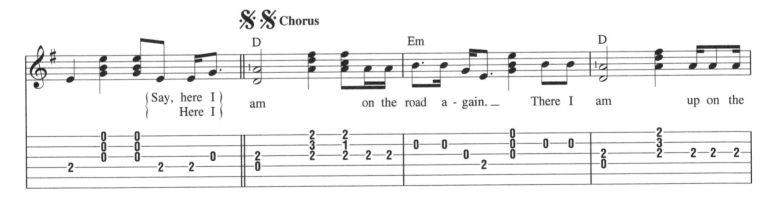

{ Say, here I } am on the road a - gain. ___ There I am up on the
{ Here I }

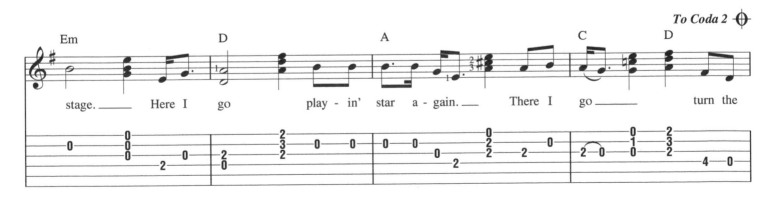

stage. ___ Here I go play - in' star a - gain. ___ There I go ___ turn the

page. _____

3. Well, you

page. _____

*D.S. al Coda 1*

**⊕ Coda 1**

mu - sic that you play. _____

6. Lat - er in the eve - ning as you

*One strum per chord, next 8 meas.

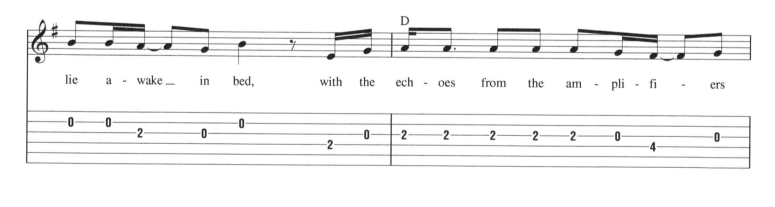

lie a - wake _ in bed, with the ech - oes from the am - pli - fi - ers

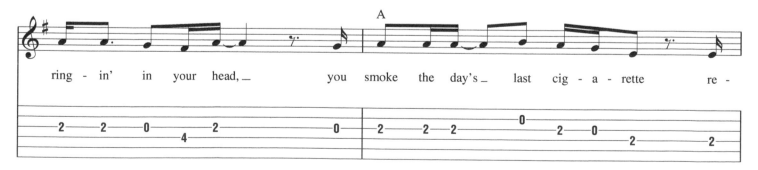

ring - in' in your head, _ you smoke the day's _ last cig - a - rette re -

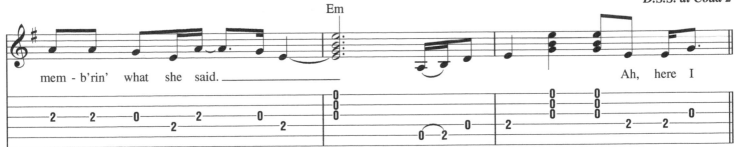

mem - b'rin' what she said. _____ Ah, here I

**⊕ Coda 2**

**Outro-Chorus**

page. _____ Ah, here I am _____ on the road a - gain. _____ There I

am up on _____ a stage. Here I go _____ play - in'

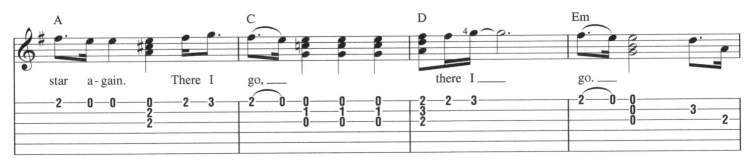

star a-gain. There I go, _____ there I _____ go. _____

*rit.*

*Additional Lyrics*

3. Well, you walk into a restaurant, strung out from the road,
   And you feel the eyes upon you as you're shakin' off the cold,
   You pretend it doesn't bother you, but you just want to explode.

4. Most times you can't hear 'em talk, other times you can.
   All the same old clichés, "Is that a woman or a man?"
   And you always seem outnumbered, you don't dare make a stand.

5. Out there in the spotlight, you're a million miles away,
   Every ounce of energy, you try to give away,
   As the sweat pours out your body like the music that you play.

# Wonderful Tonight

**Words and Music by Eric Clapton**

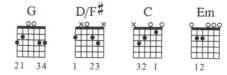

**Strum Pattern: 3, 4**
**Pick Pattern: 3, 4**

**Intro**
**Moderately slow**

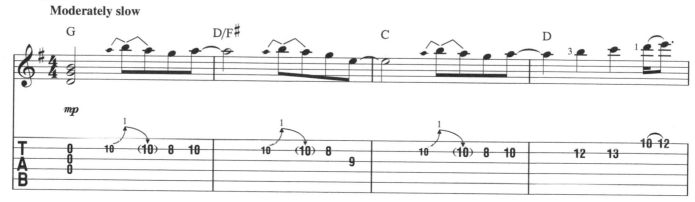

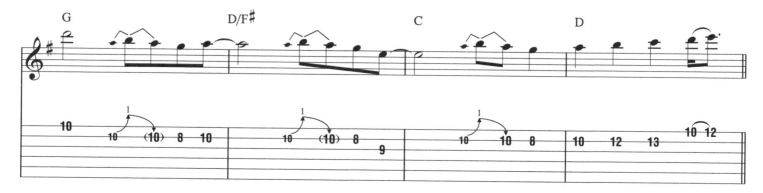

1. It's late in the eve - ning. ___ She's won-d'ring what clothes ___ to wear. ___
2., 3. *See additional lyrics*

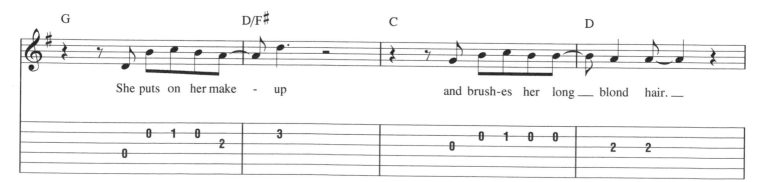

She puts on her make - up and brush-es her long ___ blond hair. ___

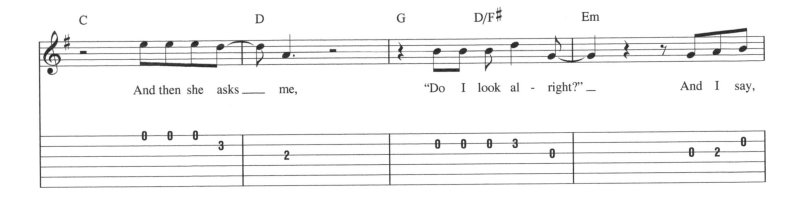

And then she asks ___ me, "Do I look al - right?" ___ And I say,

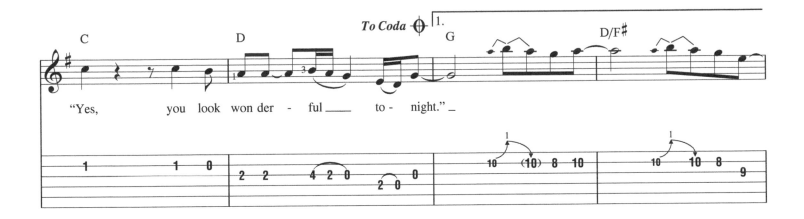

"Yes, you look won - der - ful ___ to - night." ___

I feel

**Bridge**

won - der - ful ___ be - cause I see ___ the love ___ light in ___ your ___ eyes. ___ And the

won-der of it all _____ is that you just don't re - al - ize _____ how much _ I love _

**Interlude**

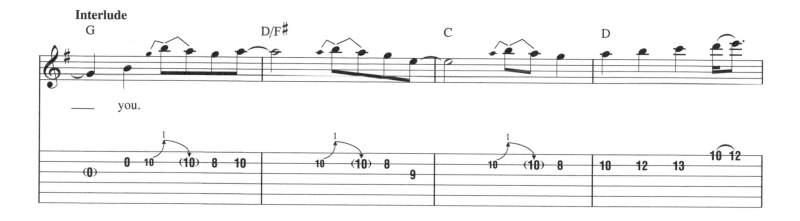

_____ you.

*D.S. al Coda*

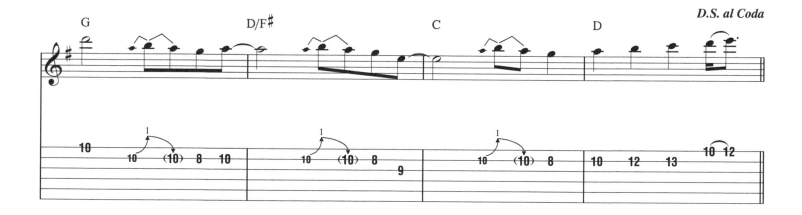

**Coda**

Oh my dar - lin', you were

**Outro**

won - der - ful _____ to - night. _____

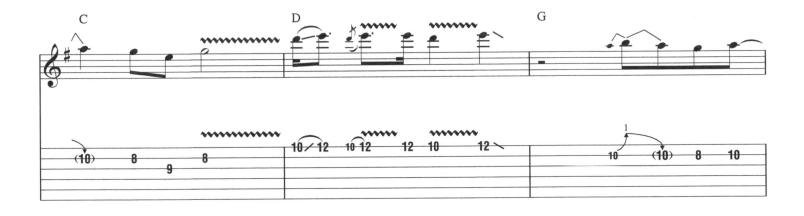

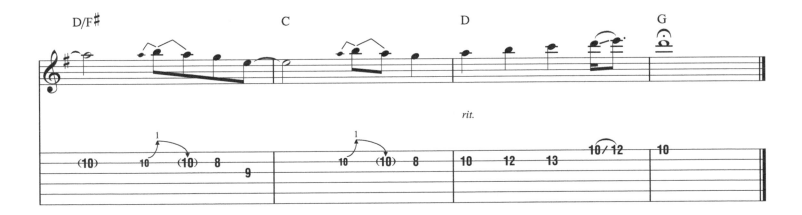

*rit.*

*Additional Lyrics*

2. We go to a party, and ev'ryone turns to see
   This beautfiul lady that's walking around with me.
   And then she asks me, "Do you feel alright?"
   And I say, "Yes, I feel wonderful tonight."

3. It's time to go home now, and I've got an aching head.
   So I give her the car keys and she helps me to bed.
   And then I tell her, as I turn out the light,
   I say, "My darling, you were wonderful tonight."

# EASY GUITAR WITH NOTES & TAB

*This series features simplified arrangements with notes, tab, chord charts, and strum and pick patterns.*

## MIXED FOLIOS

| | | |
|---|---|---|
| 00702287 | Acoustic | $19.99 |
| 00702002 | Acoustic Rock Hits for Easy Guitar | $17.99 |
| 00702166 | All-Time Best Guitar Collection | $29.99 |
| 00702232 | Best Acoustic Songs for Easy Guitar | $16.99 |
| 00119835 | Best Children's Songs | $16.99 |
| 00703055 | The Big Book of Nursery Rhymes & Children's Songs | $16.99 |
| 00698978 | Big Christmas Collection | $19.99 |
| 00702394 | Bluegrass Songs for Easy Guitar | $15.99 |
| 00289632 | Bohemian Rhapsody | $19.99 |
| 00703387 | Celtic Classics | $16.99 |
| 00224808 | Chart Hits of 2016-2017 | $14.99 |
| 00267383 | Chart Hits of 2017-2018 | $14.99 |
| 00334293 | Chart Hits of 2019-2020 | $16.99 |
| 00403479 | Chart Hits of 2021-2022 | $16.99 |
| 00702149 | Children's Christian Songbook | $9.99 |
| 00702028 | Christmas Classics | $9.99 |
| 00101779 | Christmas Guitar | $16.99 |
| 00702141 | Classic Rock | $8.95 |
| 00159642 | Classical Melodies | $12.99 |
| 00253933 | Disney/Pixar's Coco | $19.99 |
| 00702203 | CMT's 100 Greatest Country Songs | $34.99 |
| 00702283 | The Contemporary Christian Collection | $16.99 |
| 00196954 | Contemporary Disney | $19.99 |
| 00702239 | Country Classics for Easy Guitar | $24.99 |
| 00702257 | Easy Acoustic Guitar Songs | $17.99 |
| 00702041 | Favorite Hymns for Easy Guitar | $12.99 |
| 00222701 | Folk Pop Songs | $19.99 |
| 00126894 | Frozen | $14.99 |
| 00333922 | Frozen 2 | $14.99 |
| 00702286 | Glee | $16.99 |
| 00702160 | The Great American Country Songbook | $19.99 |
| 00702148 | Great American Gospel for Guitar | $14.99 |
| 00702050 | Great Classical Themes for Easy Guitar | $9.99 |
| 00148030 | Halloween Guitar Songs | $17.99 |
| 00702273 | Irish Songs | $14.99 |
| 00192503 | Jazz Classics for Easy Guitar | $16.99 |
| 00702275 | Jazz Favorites for Easy Guitar | $17.99 |
| 00702274 | Jazz Standards for Easy Guitar | $19.99 |
| 00702162 | Jumbo Easy Guitar Songbook | $24.99 |
| 00232285 | La La Land | $16.99 |
| 00702258 | Legends of Rock | $14.99 |
| 00702189 | MTV's 100 Greatest Pop Songs | $34.99 |
| 00702272 | 1950s Rock | $16.99 |
| 00702271 | 1960s Rock | $16.99 |
| 00702270 | 1970s Rock | $24.99 |
| 00702269 | 1980s Rock | $16.99 |
| 00702268 | 1990s Rock | $24.99 |
| 00369043 | Rock Songs for Kids | $14.99 |
| 00109725 | Once | $14.99 |
| 00702187 | Selections from O Brother Where Art Thou? | $19.99 |
| 00702178 | 100 Songs for Kids | $16.99 |
| 00702515 | Pirates of the Caribbean | $17.99 |
| 00702125 | Praise and Worship for Guitar | $14.99 |
| 00287930 | Songs from *A Star Is Born, The Greatest Showman, La La Land*, and More Movie Musicals | $16.99 |
| 00702285 | Southern Rock Hits | $12.99 |
| 00156420 | Star Wars Music | $16.99 |
| 00121535 | 30 Easy Celtic Guitar Solos | $16.99 |
| 00244654 | Top Hits of 2017 | $14.99 |
| 00283786 | Top Hits of 2018 | $14.99 |
| 00302269 | Top Hits of 2019 | $14.99 |
| 00355779 | Top Hits of 2020 | $14.99 |
| 00374083 | Top Hits of 2021 | $16.99 |
| 00702294 | Top Worship Hits | $17.99 |
| 00702255 | VH1's 100 Greatest Hard Rock Songs | $39.99 |
| 00702175 | VH1's 100 Greatest Songs of Rock and Roll | $34.99 |
| 00702253 | Wicked | $12.99 |

## ARTIST COLLECTIONS

| | | |
|---|---|---|
| 00702267 | AC/DC for Easy Guitar | $17.99 |
| 00156221 | Adele – 25 | $16.99 |
| 00396889 | Adele – 30 | $19.99 |
| 00702040 | Best of the Allman Brothers | $16.99 |
| 00702865 | J.S. Bach for Easy Guitar | $15.99 |
| 00702169 | Best of The Beach Boys | $16.99 |
| 00702292 | The Beatles — 1 | $22.99 |
| 00125796 | Best of Chuck Berry | $16.99 |
| 00702201 | The Essential Black Sabbath | $15.99 |
| 00702250 | blink-182 — Greatest Hits | $19.99 |
| 02501615 | Zac Brown Band — The Foundation | $19.99 |
| 02501621 | Zac Brown Band — You Get What You Give | $16.99 |
| 00702043 | Best of Johnny Cash | $19.99 |
| 00702090 | Eric Clapton's Best | $16.99 |
| 00702086 | Eric Clapton — from the Album Unplugged | $17.99 |
| 00702202 | The Essential Eric Clapton | $19.99 |
| 00702053 | Best of Patsy Cline | $17.99 |
| 00222697 | Very Best of Coldplay – 2nd Edition | $17.99 |
| 00702229 | The Very Best of Creedence Clearwater Revival | $16.99 |
| 00702145 | Best of Jim Croce | $16.99 |
| 00702278 | Crosby, Stills & Nash | $12.99 |
| 14042809 | Bob Dylan | $15.99 |
| 00702276 | Fleetwood Mac — Easy Guitar Collection | $17.99 |
| 00139462 | The Very Best of Grateful Dead | $17.99 |
| 00702136 | Best of Merle Haggard | $19.99 |
| 00702227 | Jimi Hendrix — Smash Hits | $19.99 |
| 00702288 | Best of Hillsong United | $12.99 |
| 00702236 | Best of Antonio Carlos Jobim | $15.99 |
| 00702245 | Elton John — Greatest Hits 1970–2002 | $19.99 |
| 00129855 | Jack Johnson | $17.99 |
| 00702204 | Robert Johnson | $16.99 |
| 00702234 | Selections from Toby Keith — 35 Biggest Hits | $12.95 |
| 00702003 | Kiss | $16.99 |
| 00702216 | Lynyrd Skynyrd | $17.99 |
| 00702182 | The Essential Bob Marley | $17.99 |
| 00146081 | Maroon 5 | $14.99 |
| 00121925 | Bruno Mars – Unorthodox Jukebox | $12.99 |
| 00702248 | Paul McCartney — All the Best | $14.99 |
| 00125484 | The Best of MercyMe | $12.99 |
| 00702209 | Steve Miller Band — Young Hearts (Greatest Hits) | $12.95 |
| 00124167 | Jason Mraz | $15.99 |
| 00702096 | Best of Nirvana | $17.99 |
| 00702211 | The Offspring — Greatest Hits | $17.99 |
| 00138026 | One Direction | $17.99 |
| 00702030 | Best of Roy Orbison | $17.99 |
| 00702144 | Best of Ozzy Osbourne | $14.99 |
| 00702279 | Tom Petty | $17.99 |
| 00102911 | Pink Floyd | $17.99 |
| 00702139 | Elvis Country Favorites | $19.99 |
| 00702293 | The Very Best of Prince | $22.99 |
| 00699415 | Best of Queen for Guitar | $16.99 |
| 00109279 | Best of R.E.M. | $14.99 |
| 00702208 | Red Hot Chili Peppers — Greatest Hits | $19.99 |
| 00198960 | The Rolling Stones | $17.99 |
| 00174793 | The Very Best of Santana | $16.99 |
| 00702196 | Best of Bob Seger | $16.99 |
| 00146046 | Ed Sheeran | $19.99 |
| 00702252 | Frank Sinatra — Nothing But the Best | $12.99 |
| 00702010 | Best of Rod Stewart | $17.99 |
| 00702049 | Best of George Strait | $17.99 |
| 00702259 | Taylor Swift for Easy Guitar | $15.99 |
| 00359800 | Taylor Swift – Easy Guitar Anthology | $24.99 |
| 00702260 | Taylor Swift — Fearless | $14.99 |
| 00139727 | Taylor Swift — 1989 | $19.99 |
| 00115960 | Taylor Swift — Red | $16.99 |
| 00253667 | Taylor Swift — Reputation | $17.99 |
| 00702290 | Taylor Swift — Speak Now | $16.99 |
| 00232849 | Chris Tomlin Collection – 2nd Edition | $14.99 |
| 00702226 | Chris Tomlin — See the Morning | $12.95 |
| 00148643 | Train | $14.99 |
| 00702427 | U2 — 18 Singles | $19.99 |
| 00702108 | Best of Stevie Ray Vaughan | $17.99 |
| 00279005 | The Who | $14.99 |
| 00702123 | Best of Hank Williams | $15.99 |
| 00194548 | Best of John Williams | $14.99 |
| 00702228 | Neil Young — Greatest Hits | $17.99 |
| 00119133 | Neil Young — Harvest | $16.99 |

Prices, contents and availability subject to change without notice.

Visit Hal Leonard online at halleonard.com